DAVID CAMERON became Prime Min
age of 43, the youngest PM since Lo
following the assasination of his pre
1812. He was first elected to Parliament as the Member for Witney in 2001. Educated at Eton and Oxford, he currently lives in Downing Street, SW1 next door to his good friend George.

OWEN DUDLEY EDWARDS is Hon. Fellow of the School of History, Classics and Archaeology, at the University of Edinburgh where he taught History from 1968, having been born in Ireland and studied in the USA. His wife Bonnie is American and his three children are Scots. His most recent major monograph is *British Children's Fiction in the Second World War*, his most recent collaboration *Tartan Pimps*, and he has edited several books including *A Claim of Right for Scotland*.

BOB DEWAR was born in Edinburgh and published his first illustrations at the age of 16. He went on to ghost Dennis the Menace and to work on *The Scotsman*. He has since illustrated many books, worked for many newspapers, held exhibitions and had caricatures hung in the House of Commons, among other places.

Dave Does
the Right Thing

Introduced by
OWEN DUDLEY EDWARDS

Illustrations by
BOB DEWAR

Luath Press Limited
EDINBURGH
www.luath.co.uk

First published 2014

ISBN: 978-1-910021-63-7

The paper used in this book is recyclable. It is made from
low chlorine pulps produced in a low energy, low emissions manner
from renewable forests.

Printed and bound by
CPI Antony Rowe, Chippenham

Typeset in Quadraat and MetaPlus
by 3btype.com

Contents

Foreword

You are mistaken, my friend, if you think that a man who is worth anything ought to spend his time weighing up the prospects of life and death. He has only one thing to consider in performing any action – that is, whether he is acting rightly or wrongly, like a good man or a bad one – Socrates, in Plato's *Apology*

Introduction

OWEN DUDLEY EDWARDS

Mr David Cameron appears to be busy with other matters, and so we have not troubled him to introduce this collection. My own credential is that I am writing a book for the same publishers, Messrs Luath Press, of Edinburgh, called *How David Cameron Saved Scotland*, whose findings I will not anticipate here. It should be available for Christmas 2014, rounding off what has been an interesting year for Mr Cameron and, incidentally, for the rest of us.

Our publishers, with that altruistic service to society which dominates their every action, have isolated what seems to be Mr Cameron's political signature-tune, and present fascinating contexts in which it has continually and consistently come to his aid. There are famous precedents for such things, H.H. Asquith's 'We had better wait and see' used continually in 1910 when, as Liberal Prime Minister, he faced

down furious Tories with his successful intent to destroy the House of Lords' veto over Commons legislation. The great liberal idol, W.E. Gladstone declared at Carnarvon on 10 April 1888 'We are part of the community of Europe, and we must do our duty as such', repeated (whether sarcastically or appreciatively) by the then Prime Minister, the third Marquess of Salisbury. Perhaps Mr Cameron might think of repeating it in his turn, assuming (of course) that he thinks it is the right thing.

My own earliest recollection of 'The Right Thing' was in the movie *The Mouse that Roared* (1959) where a tiny European country, Grand Fenwick, ruled by a Grand Duchess (Peter Sellers), is led by its duplicitous Prime Minister (Peter Sellers) to invade the USA so as to be defeated and reap the economic benefits of American occupation. But the brave leader (Peter Sellers) of the tiny army accidentally wins the war by capturing the latest product in nuclear bombs, its maker and his daughter, who reasons with the invaders 'Give it back! It's the right thing to do! It's the *American* thing to do!' Maybe my resurrection of these lines might tempt Mr Cameron to return Trident to the Americans, as we Scots were trying to make him do through the referendum on independence earlier this year. It would be both the right thing, and the American thing, since the thing was originally American and can only be controlled by Americans. If he doesn't, he is unlikely to find that Scots will ever regard Trident itself as The Right Thing.

All quotes are taken from speeches by and answers to questions put to David Cameron in the House of Commons, recorded in Hansard, the official record of exchanges in Parliament since 1909, unless otherwise stated.

1

Dave Does the Right Thing
for Britain

'... morality consists in the relation of actions to the rule of right; and they are denominated good or ill, according as they agree or disagree with it. What then is this rule of right? In what does it consist? How is it determined?'

DAVID HUME
An Inquiry Concerning the Principals of Morals,
1777

'I am optimistic about human nature. That's why I will trust people to do *the right thing*.'

FIRST SPEECH TO CONSERVATIVE PARTY CONFERENCE, 1 OCT 2006

'What I will do, is my duty. Which is to support the Government when they do *the right thing*. And hold them to account when they're getting it wrong.'

SECOND SPEECH TO CONSERVATIVE PARTY CONFERENCE, 1 OCT 2006

On how to deal with the European Court of Human Rights' decision to grant convicted prisoners the right to vote

'Are we going to delay and delay and waste another £160 million of taxpayers' money, or are we going to take difficult action and explain it to the British public as best we can? I do not think that we have a choice if we are to do *the right thing* and save the Exchequer money.'

3 NOV 2010: COLUMN 922

On Europe

'We should do what is in our national interest – rather than thinking that *the right thing* to do is to sign up whether or not it suits us.'

12 DEC 2011: COLUMN 527

On rejecting the EU Treaty

'The key issue for me was not whether this would be popular today, tomorrow or next week, but what was *the right thing* for Britain... I think I did *the right thing*.'

12 DEC 2011: COLUMN 535

On the Queen's Speech

'Let me say exactly what this Queen's Speech is about. It is about a Government making the tough, long-term decisions to restore our country to strength – dealing with the deficit, rebalancing the economy, and building a society that rewards people who work hard and do *the right thing*.'

9 MAY 2012: COLUMN 21

DAVE DOES THE RIGHT THING

On a recalibration of EU/UK relations

'I can confirm that that is exactly what I believe this country should do. It is *the right thing* for Britain...'

9 JAN 2013: COLUMN 309

Making the case for reducing the size of the regular army by 20,000

'It is *the right thing* to do because what is most important is to make sure that our armed forces have the best equipment of any armed forces anywhere in the world.'

2 APR 2014: COLUMN 879

On the Budget, employment, and social mobility

'...this Government have been absolutely clear that *the right thing* to do is to get stuck in to seek the best possible guarantees on British jobs, British investment and British science.'

14 MAY 2014: COLUMN 744

From a debate on Europe

'I thank my right hon. Friend for his remarks. I think that the Opposition were rather hoping that we would all be falling out over the European issue, but they can see that we are absolutely united in doing *the right thing* for Britain.'

30 JUN 2014: COLUMN 607

2

Dave Does the
Right Thing Abroad

'... the heart must be fixed on the right thing: the moment we have a fixed heart we have a free hand... We have to feel the universe at once as an ogre's castle, to be stormed, and yet as our own cottage, to which we can return at evening.'

G.K. CHESTERTON
Orthodoxy, 1908

On the UN Security Council's decision not to deploy ground troops in Libya

'We are talking about taking action to protect civilian life, and I think that is *the right thing* to do… just because we cannot do *the right thing* everywhere does not mean we should not do it when we have clear permission for and a national interest in doing so.'

21 MAR 2011: COLUMN 703–8

On counter-insurgency in Afghanistan

'The right hon. Gentleman [Ed Miliband] asks how we can increase the urgency of a political settlement. That is absolutely *the right thing* to do.'

3 MAY 2011: COLUMN 457

On the European Council's decision to reduce the regulatory burden on small to medium sized businesses

'That mirrors what we are doing in Britain, and it is *the right thing* to do.'

27 JUN 2011: COLUMN 616

On the suspension of sanctions against Burma

'That would be *the right thing* in demonstrating to the regime that we want to back progress, and it would also strongly support what Aung San Suu Kyi has said is the right approach.'

18 APR 2012: COLUMN 317

On the UK's role in Europe

'What is required often in Europe is not institutional structures, but political will to come together and do *the right thing*.'

2 JULY 2012: COLUMN 597

On the UK and Europe

'I can confirm that that is exactly what I believe this country should do. It is *the right thing* for Britain, because it is *the right thing* that we are involved in the single market and are active players in the EU.'

9 JAN 2013: COLUMN 309

DAVE DOES THE RIGHT THING

On UK/Algerian relations

'British citizens live and work all over the world and... they are working hard to do *the right things* and we should support them in that.'

18 JAN 2013: COLUMN 1171

On International Security

'I do not accept that *the right thing* to do is in any way to turn our back on the world.'

21 JAN 2013: COLUMN 34

On the humanitarian crisis and chemical warfare in Syria

'The answer is that we must do *the right thing* and in the right way.'

29 AUG 2013: COLUMN 1439

On Sri Lanka

'If he is concerned about the rights of Tamils, as I am, and reconciliation, *the right thing* to do is to go and shine a spotlight on their plight.'

18 NOV 2013: COLUMN 963

On the Commonwealth

'Britain is in the forefront of doing *the right thing* internationally.'

18 NOV 2013: COLUMN 976

On UK intervention in the Syrian civil war

'First, on Syria, I think we are doing *the right thing*, which is that we are working with the legitimate opposition – we are giving them support and giving them help, but we draw up short of lethal equipment. But there is plenty we can do to help, to train, to advise and to assist, alongside the Americans, that will make a difference and bolster those voices of democracy and freedom for the Syrian people.'

11 JUN 2014: COLUMN 554

3

Doing the Right Thing: Welfare

'In fact, it is absolutely impossible to make out by experience with complete certainty a single case in which the maxim of an action, however right in itself, rested simply on moral grounds and on the conception of duty. Sometimes it happens that with the sharpest self-examination we can find nothing beside the moral principle of duty which could have been powerful enough to move us to this or that action and to so great a sacrifice; yet we cannot from this infer with certainty that it was not really some secret impulse of self-love, under the false appearance of duty, that was the actual determining cause of the will. We like them to flatter ourselves by falsely taking credit for a more noble motive; whereas in fact we can never, even by the strictest examination, get completely behind the secret springs of action; since, when the question is of moral worth, it is not with the actions which we see that we are concerned, but with those inward principles of them which we do not see.'

IMMANUEL KANT
Fundamental Principles of the Metaphysic of Morals, 1785
TRANS. THOMAS KINGSMILL ABBOT, 1895

On housing benefits in Central London

'The housing benefit situation, particularly in central London, has got completely out of control. The idea that a family should be able to claim £2,000 a week for their house is an outrage for people who go to work every day, pay their taxes and try to do *the right thing* for their family.'

14 JULY 2010: COLUMN 949

On welfare reform

'Welfare costs have got out of control in our country. We want to ensure that work always pays, and that if people do *the right thing* we will be on their side... if you are in favour of welfare reform, and if you want to encourage people to do *the right thing*, it is no good talking about it: you have got to vote for it.'

15 JUN 2011: COLUMN 769

On student loans

'We propose that people who pay back, say, £3,000 a year in earnings should not be discouraged, because in many ways that is *the right thing to do*.'

6 JULY 2011: COLUMN 1508

On welfare reform

'...What people want is a welfare system that helps people who want to put in, work hard and do *the right thing*.'

12 OCT 2011: COLUMN 330

On the benefit cap

'Let me say this about the benefit cap. We owe it to people who work hard, do *the right thing* and pay their taxes to make sure there are some limits on welfare.'

18 JAN 2012: COLUMN 743

Reply to Ed Miliband concerning fuel prices

'Does the right hon. Gentleman support stopping the fuel increase? Yes? Then why not get up and congratulate the Government on being on the side of the motorist and the people who work hard and do *the right thing*? [...] Labour Members should be congratulating us on being on the side of those who work hard and do *the right thing*.'

27 JUN 2012: COLUMN 297

On the public response to the 'bedroom tax'

'What they say to me is that they want a Government who are on the side of people who work hard and do *the right thing*. They support the fact that we are capping welfare, getting on top of immigration and clearing up the mess left by the hon. Lady's party [Labour].'

6 FEB 2013: COLUMN 272

DAVE DOES THE RIGHT THING

On immigration and the welfare cap

'I have RAF Brize-Norton in my constituency, and many forces families live there. What they say to me is that they want a Government who are on the side of people who work hard and do *the right thing*. They support the fact that we are capping welfare, getting on top of immigration and clearing up the mess left by the hon. Lady's party [Julie Hilling, member for Bolton West, Labour].'

6 FEB 2013: COLUMN 272

On wealth inequality

'I am absolutely determined to make sure that everyone who wants to work hard and do *the right thing* can benefit from the economic recovery now under way.'

11 JUN 2014: COLUMN 546

4

The Economy

'A few theologians say that the divine emperor Antonine was not virtuous; that he was a stubborn Stoic who, not content with commanding men, wished further to be esteemed by them; that he attributed to himself the good he did to the human race; that all his life he was just, laborious, beneficent through vanity, and that lie only deceived men through his virtues. "My God!" I exclaim. "Give us often rogues like him!"'

VOLTAIRE
Philosophical Dictionary – 'VIRTUE', 1764
TRANS. H.I. WOOLF, 1924

On cutting the deficit

'Every other country is having to take this sort of action, including painful action. The right hon. and learned Lady... should talk some sense and recognise that we have to get our deficit in order, we have to take action and it is *the right thing* to do.'

21 JUN 2010: COLUMN 40

Replying to Ed Miliband on government tax and spending plans

'The question for the Government is this: in an uncertain world economy, are we taking the British economy out of the danger zone? Are we doing *the right thing* to protect the long-term interests of people's jobs and livelihoods? That is what we are doing.'

20 OCT 2010: COLUMN 940

On welfare and tax reform

'Above all, I think that *the right thing* to do is to cut the taxes of people who are in work...'

12 DEC 2012: COLUMN 294

On the Budget

'I do not think it is entirely fair to say that *the right things* were not increased or that *the right things* were not cut.'

11 FEB 2013: COLUMN 573

On a private sector-led recovery's potential to reduce youth unemployment

'As I said, there is absolutely no complacency, when more work needs to be done to make sure that this recovery delivers for people who work hard and do *the right thing*.'

11 SEP 2013: COLUMN 975

On childcare

'We are also introducing for the first time proper tax relief on child care, so that people who work hard and do *the right thing* can get help with their child care.'

9 OCT 2013: COLUMN 159

5

People Who Work Hard

'The temperate man... neither enjoys the things that the self-indulgent man enjoys most – but rather dislikes them – nor in general the things that he should not... the temperate man is not that sort of person, but the sort of person that the right rule prescribes.'

ARISTOTLE
Nicomachean Ethics, C. 350 BCE
TRANS. W.D. ROSS, 1908

On freezing tax increases

'It seems to me essential that, at a time of economic difficulty, we demonstrate that we are behind those people who want to work hard and do *the right thing*'

23 NOV 2011: COLUMN 296

On pension reform

'This Government are squarely on the side of people who work hard, play by the rules, and want to do *the right things* for their families.'

30 NOV 2011: COLUMN 937

On banning performance-related pay

'That is completely wrong. There are people working in offices, factories and shops around the country who want performance-related pay and who, if they meet some targets, would like to have a bonus at the end of the year. That is pro-aspiration and pro-doing *the right thing* for your family.'

1 FEB 2012: COLUMN 815

DAVE DOES THE RIGHT THING

On government duties and responsibilities

'This will be a Government on the side of people who work hard and do *the right thing*.'

9 MAY 2012: COLUMN 17

On work done in government so far

'That was just the start of clearing up the mess left by the Labour Party and demonstrating that this will be a Government on the side of people who work hard and do *the right thing*.'

9 MAY 2012: COLUMN 17

On tax and pension reform

'The Government's mission is to help families who work hard and do *the right thing*.'

9 MAY 2012: COLUMN 25

'...we back those who work hard and do the right thing.'

SPEECH AT BLUEWATER, KENT, 25 JUN 2012

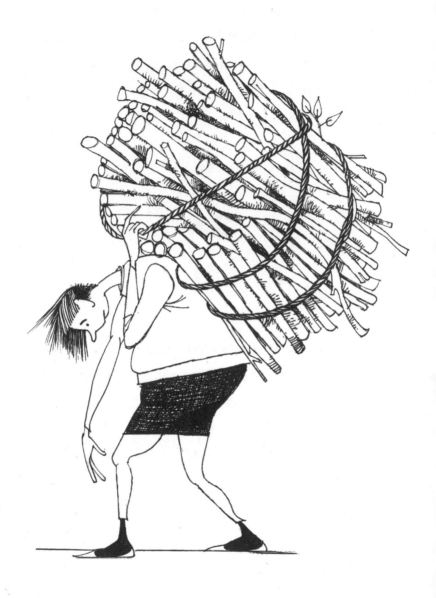

On the NHS budget

'unlike the Labour party, we are on the side of people who work hard and want to do *the right thing*.'

5 DEC 2012: COLUMN 862

On changes to the tax credit system

'we are looking at what more we can do for hard-working people who want to... do *the right thing* for their children and families.'

16 JAN 2013: COLUMN 866

DAVE DOES THE RIGHT THING

On raising the tax threshold

'the tax bill for someone on the minimum wage working full time has been cut by one half. That is a huge change to help people who work hard and want to do *the right thing*.'

6 FEB 2013: COLUMN 276

On the 'bedroom tax'

'The fact is that the public can see that we are on the side of people who work hard and want to do *the right thing*.'

6 FEB 2013: COLUMN 270

On childcare

'we will be helping people who work hard, who want to do *the right thing* and who want child care for their children...'

13 MAR 2013: COLUMN 304

On the UK and China

'We are in a global race and the way we will win is by backing families who want to work hard and do *the right thing*.'

8 MAY 2013: COLUMN 22

On the Queen's speech

'At the heart of the Queen's Speech is a commitment to get behind the aspiration of people who work hard, save hard and do *the right thing*.'

8 MAY 2013: COLUMN 25

On pension reform

'We have the priorities to stand up for people who have worked hard, done *the right thing* and saved during their lives and who deserve dignity in retirement. Unlike the Labour party, we will never let our pensioners down.'

16 OCT 2013: COLUMN 739

On pension reform

'It is absolutely vital that we say to Britain's pensioners, "You have worked hard and done *the right thing*, and we want to give you dignity and security in old age."'

8 JAN 2014: COLUMN 300

'I am absolutely determined to make sure that everyone who wants to work hard and do the right thing can benefit from the economic recovery now under way.'

11 JUN 2014: COLUMN 546

'Those who do *the right thing*, put the effort in, who work and build communities – these are the people who should be rewarded.'

SPEECH TO CONSERVATIVE PARTY CONFERENCE, 1 OCT 2014

6

The Path of Righteous Dave is Beset on All Sides

'For instance, both fear and
confidence and appetite and
anger and pity and in general
pleasure and pain may be felt
both too much and too little, and
in both cases not well; but to
feel them at the right times,
with reference to the right
objects, towards the right
people, with the right motive,
and in the right way, is what is
both intermediate and best, and
this is characteristic of virtue.'

ARISTOTLE
Nicomachean Ethics, C. 350 BCE
TRANS. W.D. ROSS, 1908

'Go with your conviction, not calculation. The popular thing may look good for a while. *The right thing* will be right all the time.'

SPEECH TO CONSERVATIVE PARTY CONFERENCE, 1 OCT 2008

'Try the big thing. Do *the right thing*. Succeed and you can really achieve something. Fail and, well, at least you tried.'

SPEECH TO CONSERVATIVE PARTY CONFERENCE, 6 OCT 2010

On the government's relationship with the media

'We have to have relationships so that politicians can try to persuade media organisations that they are trying to do *the right thing*.'

13 JUL 2011: COLUMN 325

On opting out of the EU treaty

'It was not an easy thing to do, but it was *the right thing* to do.'

12 DEC 2011: COLUMN 520

On restructuring the NHS

'Of course if you introduce choice, transparency and competition and say that the private and voluntary sectors should play a greater role you face a challenge, but that is what doing *the right thing* is sometimes all about.'

25 JAN 2012: COLUMN 294

On Ed Miliband's approach to budget cuts

'He would not do any of those things, so his cuts would be deeper, because he does not have the courage to do *the right thing*.'

16 MAY 2012: COLUMN 541

On proposed changes to UK extradition treaties

'We will ensure that we do *the right thing* for our country, but people should not think that it is a very simple issue, because it is not.'

27 JUN 2012: COLUMN 306

Diana Johnson MP, quoting David Cameron on the subject of introducing a minimum unit price for alcohol

'I know this won't be universally popular. But the responsibility of being in government isn't always about doing the popular thing. It's about doing *the right thing*.'

17 JUL 2013: COLUMN 1114

On increasing the number of UK food banks

'The Labour Government might not have wanted to do that because it was bad publicity; we did it because it was *the right thing*.'

4 SEP 2013: COLUMN 311

On UK military involvement in Syria

'The fact is that Opposition Front Benchers are wriggling and quibbling because they know they had a choice. They could have done the difficult thing and *the right thing* for the country; instead, they chose the easy and simple thing that was politically convenient.'

9 SEP 2013: COLUMN 697

On allowing job centres to refer people to food banks

'Labour did not do it because it was bad PR, but this Government are interested in doing *the right thing* rather than something that just looks good.'

11 SEP 2013: COLUMN 975

On taking action against payday lenders

'I feel like one of those radio hosts who say, "And your complaint is, caller, exactly?" We are doing *the right thing*. The right hon. Gentleman should stand up and congratulate us.'

27 NOV 2013: COLUMN 251

On increasing the number of food banks in the UK

'It is important to do *the right thing* rather than something that might just seem politically convenient.'

22 JAN 2014: COLUMN 290

On the prospect of further cuts

'Difficult decisions on public service pay and pensions, further savings in Departments, a cap on welfare bills – none of these decisions is easy, but they are *the right thing* to ensure that Britain lives within her means.'

19 MAR 2014: COLUMN 785

On the aftermath of the expenses scandal

'I hope the one lesson that will not be learned is that *the right thing* to do as soon as someone has to answer allegations is just to remove them instantly, rather than give them a chance to clear their name and get on with their job.'

9 APR 2014: COLUMN 257

In reply to Ed Miliband on the prospect of using the public interest test on Pfizer's take-over bid for AstraZeneca

'Does it not tell us everything that, given the choice of doing *the right thing* for the national interest and working with the Government or making short-term political points, that is what he chooses to do?'

7 MAY 2014: COLUMN 146

1

Why? Just Because...

'... it is the particular RIGHT OF MASTERS to create values...'

FRIEDRICH NIETZSCHE
Beyond Good and Evil, 1886
TRANS. HELEN ZIMMERN, 1913

On the Prime Minister's failure to mention Nobel peace laureate Liu Xiaobo in talks with the Chinese government

'What I did, which was *the right thing* to do, was to have a very frank exchange about human rights with the Chinese in the meetings that we had…'

15 NOV 2010: COLUMN 650

On the UN Security Council Resolution on Libya

'I absolutely believe that that is *the right thing* both to say and to do.'

18 MAR 2011: COLUMN 612

On equalisation of the pension age between men and women

'I think that is a good deal and *the right thing* to do.'

15 JUN 2011: COLUMN 773

On NATO operations in Libya

'I had a meeting with the First Sea Lord yesterday at which he agreed that we can sustain the mission for as long as we need to, and those were exactly the words that the Chief of the Defence Staff used yesterday, because we are doing *the right thing*.'

15 JUN 2011: COLUMN 777

DAVE DOES THE RIGHT THING

On the winter fuel allowance

'we have kept the plans that were set out by the previous Government and I think that is *the right thing* to do.'

2 NOV 2011: COLUMN 918

On seeking safeguards for Britain during a Eurozone crisis

'That is *the right thing* to do.'

7 DEC 2011: COLUMN 293

On increasing the NHS budget

'We do not think it is irresponsible; we think it is *the right thing* to do.'

7 DEC 2011: COLUMN 300

'This is quite simply about doing *the right thing*...'

SPEECH AT BLUEWATER, KENT, 25 JUN 2012

On the EU treaty referendum

'What matters is doing *the right thing*.'

2 JUL 2012: COLUMN 593

On the banking scandal

'I want an inquiry to be completed... I think that that is *the right thing* to do.'

2 JUL 2012: COLUMN 590

On increasing the NHS budget, again

'The Opposition and he believe that increasing spending on the NHS is irresponsible; we think it is *the right thing* to do.'

21 NOV 2012: COLUMN 574

On the decision to lift the Syrian arms embargo

'That was *the right thing* to do.'

3 JUN 2013: COLUMN 1242

On youth unemployment

'As we stand today, employment is growing faster here than it is in any other G7 country, including Germany, so we are doing *the right thing*.'

26 JUN 2013: COLUMN 299

On attention paid to public opinion on international affairs

'That is *the right thing* for the Government to do and we will continue to do it.'

29 AUG 2013: COLUMN 1428

On capping payday lenders

'We have looked at a cap. We have looked at the evidence from Australia, Florida and elsewhere. It is *the right thing* to do and I am proud that we are doing it.'

27 NOV 2013: COLUMN 251

On the withdrawal of British troops from Afghanistan

'If we are going to take steps – diplomatically, politically and, potentially, economically – we should take them because it is *the right thing* to do.'

10 MAR 2014: COLUMN 33

In response to a question about ambulance waiting times

'I am very happy to look at the case the hon. Lady mentions. She says she does not want that, but I think that is *the right thing* to do...'

26 MAR 2014: COLUMN 343

On defence cuts and national security

'We will review the national security strategy on the four-year rolling basis that we established it – that is *the right thing* to do.'

26 MAR 2014: COLUMN 344

8

Thanks for Doing the Right Thing

'Neither is there only a habit of goodness, directed by right reason; but there is in some men, even in nature, a disposition towards it; as on the other side, there is a natural malignity.'

FRANCIS BACON
The Essays and Council, Civil and Moral,
1597

On the decision to retire Harrier Jump-Jets from active service

'I came at the problem as a politician quite tempted by the easy political answer, but the right military answer is *the right thing* to do for our country.'

19 OCT 2010: COLUMN 809

On teachers at Vaynor First School deciding not to strike

'I congratulate them on doing *the right thing...*'

29 JUN 2011: COLUMN 946

In reply to Ed Miliband

'...I thank him for what he said about recalling Parliament. That was the *right thing* to do.'

20 JULY 2011: COLUMN 924

On protection for war memorials and new penalties for those who attack them

'this is really important, because all of us want to do *the right thing*...'

23 NOV 2011: COLUMN 296

In reply to Conservative party member for South Ribble, Lorraine Fullbrook

'My hon. Friend is absolutely right to speak up for her constituents who work hard and do *the right thing*.'

12 SEP 2012: COLUMN 273

9

Dave is Doing the Right Thing, Right?

'Therefore it is unnecessary for a prince to have all the good qualities I have enumerated, but it is very necessary to appear to have them. And I shall dare to say this also, that to have them and always to observe them is injurious, and that to appear to have them is useful; to appear merciful, faithful, humane, religious, upright, and to be so, but with a mind so framed that should you require not to be so, you may be able and know how to change to the opposite.'

NICCOLÒ MACHIAVELLI
The Prince, 1513
TRANS. W.K. MARRIOTT, 1908

Chris Kelly (Dudley South, Conservative) on negotiations with the EU

'I congratulate my right hon. Friend on once again doing *the right thing...*'

26 NOV 2012: COLUMN 46

Ed Miliband on the Prime Minister's attitude to energy price freezes

'Can he explain why a price freeze was wrong six months ago but *the right thing* to do today?'

26 MAR 2014: COLUMN 339

Ed Miliband on Maria Miller's apology over her expenses

'The Prime Minister said six days ago that she had "done *the right thing*" and that we should "leave it at that". Does he now recognise that that was a terrible error of judgment?

9 APR 2014: COLUMN 258

Kevin Brennan (Cardiff West, Labour) on the Pfizer take-over bid for AstraZeneca

'The AstraZeneca boss said that it could put lives at risk. How could any Prime Minister worth the title not immediately conclude that *the right thing* to do in the national interest is to call this in?'

14 MAY 2014: COLUMN 748

Ed Miliband on the Leveson Enquiry

'Now it is clear from the Prime Minister – [Hon. Members: "Weak!"] I will tell them what is weak: failing to stand up for doing *the right thing*, and that is what this Prime Minister has done.'

25 JUN 2014: COLUMN 309

Mr David Nuttall (Bury North, Conservative) on negotiations with Europe

'The Prime Minister did exactly *the right thing* last week, and I congratulate him on standing up for British interests.'

30 JUN 2014: COLUMN 616

Mr Peter Bone (Wellingborough, Conservative) on the Prime Minister's recent negotiations with Europe

'Everyone we spoke to, whether they were a Conservative supporter, a Labour supporter or a Liberal Democrat supporter... all thought that the Prime Minister had done *the right thing*.'

30 JUN 2014: COLUMN 625

Ed Miliband (Leader of the Opposition)

'We have always said that we will support the Government when they do *the right thing*...'

16 JUL 2014: COLUMN 853

Lord Armstrong of Ilminster on making Lady Stowell a member of the Cabinet

'To paraphrase the old song: if you have a *right thing*, do it; do not dream it, do it now.'

28 JUL 2014: COLUMN 1501

Lord Butler of Brockwell on the same possibility

'There is still time for the Prime Minister to do *the right thing*, and I hope that he will do so.'

28 JUL 2014: COLUMN 1507

Lord Dannatt in support of the government's proposal to begin airstrikes in Iraq

'I believe the Prime Minister has done *the right thing* in carefully building support for his proposed course of action...'

26 SEP 2014: COLUMN 1694

Lord Kirkwood in the same debate

'It is correct that Governments should test parliamentary opinion by recalling both Houses. Even if they lose occasionally, it is still *the right thing* to do...'

26 SEP 2014: COLUMN 1698

Luath Press Limited
committed to publishing well written books worth reading

LUATH PRESS takes its name from Robert Burns, whose little collie Luath (*Gael.,* swift or nimble) tripped up Jean Armour at a wedding and gave him the chance to speak to the woman who was to be his wife and the abiding love of his life. Burns called one of 'The Twa Dogs' Luath after Cuchullin's hunting dog in Ossian's *Fingal.* Luath Press was established in 1981 in the heart of Burns country, and now resides a few steps up the road from Burns' first lodgings on Edinburgh's Royal Mile. Luath offers you distinctive writing with a hint of unexpected pleasures.

Most bookshops in the UK, the US, Canada, Australia, New Zealand and parts of Europe either carry our books in stock or can order them for you. To order direct from us, please send a £sterling cheque, postal order, international money order or your credit card details (number, address of cardholder and expiry date) to us at the address below. Please add post and packing as follows: UK – £1.00 per delivery address; overseas surface mail – £2.50 per delivery address; overseas airmail – £3.50 for the first book to each delivery address, plus £1.00 for each additional book by airmail to the same address. If your order is a gift, we will happily enclose your card or message at no extra charge.

Luath Press Limited
543/2 Castlehill
The Royal Mile
Edinburgh EH1 2ND
Scotland

Telephone: 0131 225 4326 (24 hours)
email: sales@luath.co.uk
Website: www.luath.co.uk